THIS JOURNAL BELONGS TO...

....

KNOW YOUR BIBLE BETTER

KNOW
YOUR
BIBLE
BETTER

A Guide & Journal
for Growing
Your Faith

BARBOUR
PUBLISHING

ISBN 979-8-89151-084-5

Published by Barbour Publishing, Inc., 1810 Barbour Drive, Uhrichsville, Ohio 44683, www.barbourbooks.com

Our mission is to inspire the world with the life-changing message of the Bible.

Printed in China.

WELCOME TO KNOW YOUR BIBLE BETTER

When you study the Bible, you'll discover what millions of people have found throughout the centuries: You're reading the Word of the living God. In times past, He spoke to His special servants audibly, in visions and in dreams; now His main method of revelation to all humanity is His written Word.

Over a period of fifteen hundred years, the Holy Spirit directed forty holy men of God, living on three continents, to write His words into sixty-six books. These writings were preserved and collected into the single volume we know as the Bible.

Though people wrote it, the Bible itself says *God* was its ultimate source. In 2 Timothy 3:16, we read, "All scripture is given by inspiration of God," which literally means it was breathed out by God.

The New Testament gives several descriptive titles to the Bible: the Word of God, the oracles of God, the Word of Christ, the holy scriptures, the word of truth, and the word of life. In studying the Bible, we're learning God's Word, holy and true, which contains the knowledge of eternal life.

To be healthy, growing Christians, we must study God's Word—and that's what this journal is all about. On the pages to follow, you'll find time-tested insights into reading, contemplating, and applying scripture, along with plenty of space afterward for you to write down observations from your own study. We hope and pray that through using this book, you'll be encouraged to become one of those believers who is taught by God, learning His Word and receiving the special blessings He's reserved for you.

Jesus Himself made it clear that learning and living the Bible is God's will for our lives. He said, "Man shall not live by bread alone, but by every word that proceeds out of the mouth of God" (Matthew 4:4). Bible study isn't just a nice thing to do—it's essential to our lives!

Using This Journal

The following 28 pages contain an abridged version of *How to Study the Bible* by Robert M. West, a helpful little book that has sold over a million copies. Read and digest this information, then use the balance of this book for capturing your own Bible study insights.

The journaling pages include prompts only for the date and topic of your study; otherwise, they are completely open for your notes, whether you're pursuing a book or word study, a character profile, or some other aspect of biblical exploration. This journal can become a permanent record of your spiritual walk, something to refer to over time to recall what God has taught you in your study of His Word.

CHAPTER 1

PREPARATION

Readying Our Hearts for Bible Study

For the word of God is living and active, and sharper than any two-edged sword, even penetrating as far as the division of soul and spirit, of both joints and marrow, and able to judge the thoughts and intentions of the heart.

HEBREWS 4:12 NASB

People who want to learn how to study the Bible often ask, "Where do I begin?"

It's a good question, but the answer might be surprising. We actually begin with ourselves. We prepare our hearts to study the Bible.

As we think about personal Bible study, we shouldn't view it as another intellectual exercise like the study of math, science, history, or anything else that interests us. When studying these disciplines, the mind is engaged, but not the heart. God wants us to increase our knowledge of His Word with our minds, but He also intends for the power of His Word to affect our hearts and that our lives will be changed to become more like Christ's.

Concern for a change of life was expressed by the Lord Jesus for His disciples when He prayed, "Sanctify them through Your truth. Your word is truth" (John 17:17).

When our minds and our hearts are prepared and involved in Bible study, our time spent in God's Word is enjoyable and exciting.

People can have a good study Bible, own some helpful study books, follow numerous recommended procedures, and have a quiet place to concentrate, and still not benefit spiritually from the time spent in the Bible because their hearts aren't prepared to be involved in the process.

This section opened with the words of Hebrews 4:12. The context of this verse reveals that God knows everything about every one of us. As we read His Word, it functions as an X-ray machine or heart monitor, revealing to us what He sees in our hearts. Let's see ourselves as God sees us. His Word exposes our hearts so we can take corrective action (Hebrews 4:13).

I suggest that preparing our hearts means two things. First, we need to approach God's Word *dependently*. Second, we need to approach God's Word *purposefully*.

DEPENDENTLY

Depend on the Holy Spirit

Many people who begin to study the Bible will soon be saying, "I need help!" That's a good conclusion to come to. We all need help, and the person to help us is God. He gave us His Word and also assists us in understanding it. The technical term for this help is *illumination*.

Paul spoke about illumination when he said, "But the natural man does not receive the things of the Spirit of God, for they are foolishness to him. Nor can he know them, because they are spiritually discerned" (1 Corinthians 2:14).

The natural man refers to someone who hasn't been saved and therefore doesn't have the indwelling Holy Spirit. Christ's Word must be understood on a spiritual level, not just an intellectual level.

The only person who can make the blind see is God, so He's the one we depend on to give us understanding of His Word. The first thing a person needs, simply put, is to be saved, to be totally dependent on God for all their spiritual needs (see Acts 16:30–31).

Once we have recognized our need for help from God to understand His Word, we should regularly pray for His assistance. The psalmist realized this and expressed dependence to God: "Open my eyes, that I may see wondrous things from Your law" (Psalm 119:18). This is a great prayer for us as well when we prepare our hearts to study His Word.

Depend on Mature Believers

Not only should we depend on the teaching ministry of the Holy Spirit, but we should also depend on mature believers who have a strong knowledge of God's Word.

According to the apostle Paul, God gives certain people a supernatural ability to teach the Word: "We have differing gifts according to the grace that is given to us: whether. . .ministry, let us attend to our ministering; or he who teaches, on teaching"(Romans 12:6–7).

But teaching occurs in many settings, as Moses told the ancient Israelites: "These words, which I am commanding you today, shall be on your heart. And you shall repeat them diligently to your sons and speak of them when you sit in your house, when you walk on the road, when you lie down, and when you get up" (Deuteronomy 6:6–7 NASB). The design of God is that mature Christians teach His Word to others.

The Holy Spirit and gifted teachers help us to understand and apply those commands to our own lives.

PURPOSEFULLY

We should be clear in our minds why we are spending part of our day studying. This is another part of personal preparation. We'd know why we were studying if we were to give a devotional message or share our thoughts about a biblical topic with a group. We'd be motivated by the specific task before us.

But what we're considering at this point are the reasons we're to be consistent in our everyday habits. What is it that motivates us to study like the Bereans in Acts 17:11, who "searched the scriptures daily"?

The best answers come straight from the Bible. Following are several reasons, directly from God's Word.

1. To settle the issue of our own salvation

Paul reminded Timothy about Timothy's own experience: "From childhood you have known the holy scriptures, which are able to make you wise for salvation through faith that is in Christ Jesus" (2 Timothy 3:15). This is the primary issue that needs to be settled in everyone's life.

God uses His Word as a means to save sinners. As we think about our conversion, we may be able to identify Bible verses that God used in our lives to save us—or at least a believer's life-giving words that were based on scripture. God also wants us to have what the hymn writer Fanny Crosby called "blessed assurance." Many Christians experience doubts about their own conversion, and through learning those portions of scripture that address this subject, we can have a deepening confidence about our own salvation.

2. To grow spiritually

New Christians are sometimes described as babes in Christ, and of course, all babies need to grow. Peter gave this instruction to Christians in the early church: "But grow in grace and in the knowledge of our Lord and Savior Jesus Christ" (2 Peter 3:18).

He also gave a direct exhortation that they should have the same kind of desire for the basic truths of God's Word that a newborn baby has for milk: "As newborn babies, desire the sincere milk of the word, that you may grow by it" (1 Peter 2:2). This is a picture representing intense hunger for God's Word so that we can grow in our understanding and spiritual strength. The Bible repeatedly refers to itself as food for the soul. Just as our bodies need food to survive, our souls need the spiritual food of the Bible.

3. To receive personal blessing and encouragement

Paul wrote, "For whatever things were written formerly were written for our learning, that through patience and comfort from the scriptures might have hope" (Romans 15:4). As believers, we often experience discouragement in our Christian walk. A common cause of this discouragement is conflict between believers, which Paul addresses in Romans 15. Difficulties between Christians, which create a lack of unity, can be discouraging. As we all eventually learn, there's no lack of tension and trouble in local churches. But as we study the Bible, we see Christ's example. How He interacted with people is the pattern we're to follow for living and for treating others.

When we study the Bible, we'll also read numerous promises God made to give believers hope, and stories about how God providentially worked in the lives of people. Meditating on all these passages of scripture encourages us to persevere in our own Christian life with comfort and hope.

4. To receive personal guidance

When faced with many of life's decisions, we often wonder, *What should I do now?* Learning the Bible can be helpful in answering this question. "Your word is a lamp to my feet and a light to my path" (Psalm 119:105).

The psalmist pictured the effect of learning God's Word as having a lamp for life that lights the way before us so we can see where we're going.

Many times, the Bible addresses our specific situation, but when it doesn't, there are principles we can apply to our lives so we have confidence that we're being led by God's Word. As we seek God's guidance, He'll lead us by His Spirit (Romans 8:14), who always agrees with what God has revealed to us in His Word. His Spirit's leading never contradicts what He's written. If our personal decisions contradict what has been written in the Bible, then we can be sure we aren't being led by God.

5. To defend ourselves against the devil

Soon after we become Christians, we find out that the Christian life involves spiritual warfare. In Ephesians 6, Paul instructs believers with these words: "Put on the whole armor of God, that you may be able to stand against the schemes of the devil" (verse 11). The schemes of the devil are the methods he uses against people while trying to keep them from doing the will of God.

The Christian's defense against this assault is to put on the spiritual armor of God: Christian character and lifestyle empowered by God's Spirit. A vital part of this armor is "the sword of the Spirit, which is the word of God" (verse 17).

Through Bible study, we'll also be able to remember specific Bible verses, and by applying them, we'll be able to overcome the devil's temptations.

6. To present ourselves approved to God

"Be diligent to present yourself approved to God as a worker who does not need to be ashamed, accurately handling the word of truth" (2 Timothy 2:15 NASB). Learning God's truth involves the work of studying.

Like divers who work to locate pearls in the ocean or miners who labor to find gold in the earth, Christians are workers who study the Bible to discover God's truth. We live our lives before God, and as servants we're to regularly present our lives to Him to be examined. We hope to have a sense of His approval and eventually hear from Him, "Well done, good and faithful servant." Divine approval comes from diligently studying God's Word so we can accurately share it with others.

INTERPRETATION

Discovering What the Bible Means

Be diligent to present yourself approved to God as a worker who does not need to be ashamed, accurately handling the word of truth.

2 TIMOTHY 2:15 NASB

Frequently people discussing the meaning of the Bible say, "Oh, that's just your interpretation." Is there a way to figure out what it means? The answer is a resounding yes! Following are a number of guidelines to help you interpret the Bible properly.

Whether we realize it or not, we all interpret the Bible whenever we try to understand its meaning and make applications to our lives. The fact that we're already doing this shows how important it is that we learn to interpret correctly.

ONE INTERPRETATION, MANY APPLICATIONS

A good thought to begin with is this: Each verse of scripture has only one intended meaning even though there may be many applications. The Bible isn't written to mean different things to different people. The issue in every verse is always what *God* means by it, not what it means to me.

When interpreting a biblical text, there are a number of things to consider. Some texts clearly apply to everyone everywhere, while other texts apply only to people in the Bible who lived in a former time. Some things are to be understood literally, and others figuratively.

Some people bring their personal circumstances to texts of scripture and may wrongly think that God is speaking directly to them in some mysterious and secret way from a particular text.

Poor interpretation comes from preconceived ideas, bad theology, being too hasty in reaching conclusions, and ignoring principles of interpretation. This is why it's so important to learn basic guidelines that help us learn what God means by what He said.

The time and work you invest will be rewarded by great discoveries of precious truth. Miners who search for gold or other precious metals keep their minds fixed on the value of the discovery they hope to make. They know they must devote time to their task. If you hear about a microwave Bible study plan—that is, a plan that lets you get it done quickly—ignore it, because it won't be that beneficial.

It's been said that the Bible wasn't written for scholars, but for sinners. It's a book for all of us. Many parts are more difficult than others, but this shouldn't discourage us. Even Peter said that some of the things written by his beloved brother Paul were hard to understand (2 Peter 3:15–16).

As we read and study the Bible, we don't have to be overly concerned by those things we don't understand. As we read God's Word daily, we will grow in understanding and be able to deal with more difficult doctrines later.

Watch Out for False Teachers

As a warning to those who want to understand God's Word, the Bible speaks of false teachers who manipulate what the Bible says and who can be a bad influence if we don't guard ourselves against them. Jesus criticized the Sadducees of His day, who denied physical resurrection. He told them, "You err, not knowing the scriptures" (Matthew 22:29). These men explained away certain Old Testament texts and spiritualized others, resulting in serious error.

Paul spoke of some religious and educated people living in the last days when he said that they are "ever learning and never able to come to the knowledge of the truth.... These also resist the truth" (2 Timothy 3:7–8).

False teachers often redefine biblical words, so we must check to make sure we understand how they are using them or God's intended meaning of verses becomes lost.

In learning to interpret scripture, we must discuss inductive Bible study, which seeks to discover the facts and details in a text and to draw conclusions about the meaning of a text from those observations. Inductive study has a sequence of three components: observation, interpretation, and application.

- Observation answers the question, *What does it say?* What is the actual content in the text?
- Interpretation answers the question, *What does it mean?* Our task is to discover the original intent and meaning of the author.
- Application answers the questions, *What does it mean to me?* and *How does it apply to my life?*

When we use this sequence, we'll find information and ideas that might have been overlooked otherwise.

Observation

Observation always comes first. Before we consider what a text *means*, we must ask what it *says*. This means reading and rereading a text until we become acquainted with it.

In developing our observation skills, we'll find it helpful to ask a series of questions. We can use them for any text. Put your text under a light and interrogate it! We just want the facts. Texts will have answers for most of the following questions:

- *Who?* Who was writing? To whom was the message originally written? Who are the people involved in the scenario?
- *What?* What's happening? What's said? Is it a command, an exhortation, a rebuke, a question, an answer, a prayer, a quotation of other scripture, or something else? What's the main point? What key words or phrases are used? What's the context? What literary style is being used? Is it narrative, conversation, parable, prophecy, poetry, a letter, or a sermon?

- *When?* Are there time references? Are there words related to the past, present, or future? Look for words like *after*, *until*, and *then*.
- *Where?* Are there locations mentioned—towns, roads, rivers, mountains, regions, or other landmarks?
- *Why?* Are there any clues about why things are being said or done?
- *How?* Is there an explanation about how things are done?

These six questions help us gain information to see what a text actually says.

Interpretation

The ultimate interpretation question is, *What did God mean by what He said?* Interpretation is determining the meaning of a text once all of the facts are in. Compiling evidence from our observation takes some time, and we must guard against jumping to premature conclusions. New evidence can influence our conclusions, so we shouldn't be too hasty in moving to this part of the inductive process.

Some of us have been in Bible study classes where the facilitator asked, "What does this passage mean to you?" before the group observed the facts and determined what the author intended. This is a good question when asked at the right time because it forces people to think about the Bible, but it's not a good question to ask first because people speak offhandedly before they give thought to the text. In this situation, interpreting the Bible becomes totally subjective, meaning different things to different people.

But every verse in the Bible means only one thing—what the original author intended—and that's what we're trying to discover. Second Timothy 2:15 (NASB) speaks of "accurately handling the word of truth." In Greek, "accurately handling" literally means "cutting a straight line." When Paul, a tentmaker, wrote to Timothy, he may have had in mind cutting material in a straight line to sew pieces of a tent together. Paul and Timothy needed to be precise and accurate in interpreting and teaching the Bible so it would all fit together without contradiction.

Once we have asked the six observation questions of the text, we then apply six principles of interpretation.

1. The Literal Principle

The literal principle means interpreting the Bible with the normal meaning of words while recognizing figures of speech like symbolism, allegory, and metaphor. God has communicated with us through written language, so we should understand the words of scripture the way we use them in everyday life. Let a text speak for itself. When Jesus was born, it was a literal virgin birth. The miracles He performed were real. His death and resurrection were actual historical events.

We recognize that many portions of scripture, especially poetry and prophecy, are filled with figurative language. Psalm 91:4 is an example of figurative language in Hebrew poetry: "He shall cover you with His feathers, and under His wings you shall trust." This doesn't mean that God has feathers and wings; rather, in it provides an image of God as our protector the same way a bird protects its young by covering them with its wings.

When the literal principle is used, the Bible is much easier to understand. There's no need to uncover hidden meanings.

2. The Historical Principle

The Bible must be understood in its historical setting before it can be fully understood in our contemporary setting. Bible students now become historians. We want to discover the original intent of the author by asking, *What did he mean by what he wrote?* Would our interpretation make sense to the first recipients? Before we ask what a text means to us, we must first ask what it meant to the original audience.

It's helpful to investigate the lifestyle and customs of that day, such as foot washing (1 Timothy 5:9–10), praying on a housetop (Acts 10:9), and girding the loins (1 Peter 1:13). Learning about the political and social backgrounds sheds light on certain texts. Bible study tools discussed in chapter 4 will prove helpful when studying historical background.

3. The Contextual Principle

The contextual principle means we should interpret a verse by the verses that surround it. You may have noticed that some verses begin in the middle of a sentence, so it's best to at least go back to the beginning of the sentence to get the flow of the author's thought.

When Satan tempted Jesus and suggested that He should throw Himself down from the top of the temple, the devil quoted Bible verses out of context, giving them a wrong meaning. A psalm about trusting God was twisted into meaning that it's all right to test God (Matthew 4:5–6 and Psalm 91:11–12). Jesus corrected the devil's error by quoting another text that rectified the wrong idea (Matthew 4:7 and Deuteronomy 6:16).

It's best to get the big picture of a text, then the context, and finally the details. This is starting with the bird's-eye view and going down to the worm's-eye view.

- Find out the general theme of the book.
- Determine the emphasis of each chapter and how it relates to the book theme.
- Find the paragraph divisions and how they relate to the thrust of each chapter.
- Dig into the verses to get each one's main idea and how they relate to each other.
- Go deeper into verses by doing word studies.

4. The Compatibility Principle

The basic premise of the compatibility principle is to compare verses or passages of scripture with other scripture to see how they fit together. The best commentary on the Bible is the Bible, so we let it interpret itself. Properly understood, the Bible doesn't contradict itself; it complements itself. If our interpretations contradict what the Bible says elsewhere, we need to change our conclusions. As we study a text or subject, other portions of scripture shed light on it for fuller understanding. For example, doctrinal truth is spread throughout the Bible.

Comparing scripture with scripture is a safeguard against error and contradiction.

5. The Grammatical Principle

Recognizing parts of speech and the way they relate to each other can reveal a lot about a biblical text. Seven easily overlooked but important words are *therefore*, *and*, *but*, *that*, *for*, *because*, and *if*. Examples of these are found in Romans 11–12.

In Romans 12:1, Paul writes, "*Therefore* I beseech you, brothers, by the mercies of God, that you present your bodies as a living sacrifice" (emphasis added). When we see the word *therefore*, we need to find out what it's there for. Find out what thoughts have gone before. In the first eleven chapters of Romans, Paul has laid the great foundation of the mercies of God by describing in detail God's plan of salvation. Paul then draws his thoughts to a practical conclusion in 12:1 and begs the Romans to present themselves to God as dedicated servants. He connects his practical appeal to his lengthy description of God's plan by the word *therefore*.

Verse 2 continues: "*And* do not be conformed to this world, *but* be transformed by the renewing of your mind, *that* you may prove what is that good and acceptable and perfect will of God." *And* introduces an addition, *but* points to a contrast, and *that* is used to begin a conclusion. Paul adds another appeal after his first one in verse 1 by using the word *and* at the beginning of verse 2. Then he presents a contrast with the word *but*. Paul exhorts believers not to succumb to external pressure to live and think like the unbelieving world, *but* to be internally transformed by renewing their thought life. (By the way, the source for renewed thinking is the Bible. See Psalm 1:1–2.)

That (along with *for* and *because*) is used to introduce a purpose or reason at the end of verse 2. The reason for having our thinking renewed and our life transformed is so we can have confidence that we know and are doing the will of God.

In verse 19, the word *for* is also used to introduce a reason: Paul has written that Christians shouldn't be vengeful *for* the scriptures say we shouldn't.

An example of the use of *because*, also meaning purpose or reason, is found in Romans 11:20: "They were broken off *because* of unbelief."

If is used in Romans 12:18: "*If* it is possible, as much as it lies in you, live peaceably with all men." This word is used when a condition is present. Paul's point here is that Christians are always to be peacemakers, and if there is a lack of peace between a Christian and another person, it should never be the Christian's fault.

Considering these seven words helps us better understand the structure and meaning of a text.

6. The Christological Principle

Jesus Christ is the main theme of the entire Bible, so keeping an eye out for references to Him as we study is important. The ministry of the Holy Spirit is to point us to Christ: "But when the Comforter comes, . . .the Spirit of truth. . . , He shall testify of Me" (John 15:26).

Jesus said to unbelieving Jews of His day, "Search the scriptures, for in them you think you have eternal life. And these are they that testify of Me. . . . For had you believed Moses, you would have believed Me, for he wrote about Me" (John 5:39, 46). Moses wrote the first five books of the Old Testament, so we look for Christ there.

At the end of His earthly ministry, Jesus told His apostles, "All things must be fulfilled that were written in the Law of Moses and in the Prophets and in the Psalms concerning Me" (Luke 24:44). Therefore, we also look for Jesus in the prophetic books and the psalms.

One day, an Ethiopian eunuch was reading the Old Testament text of Isaiah, which contains a prophecy about the Lord Jesus. A believer, Philip helped, him understand what he was reading. "Then Philip opened his mouth and, beginning at the same scripture [Isaiah 53:7–8], preached Jesus to him" (Acts 8:35). We should always be looking for Christ.

Application

Now we come to application, the third component of inductive Bible study. This answers the question, *How does this passage apply to me?* Bible study doesn't end with interpretation; it continues to the question, *So what?* The goal of Bible study isn't only gaining information but experiencing transformation. We're not just trying to get through the Bible; we're letting the Bible get through us. If there's a good example, follow it. If there's a warning, heed it. If there's a command, obey it. If there's a promise, believe it.

Jesus prayed for all believers just before He died: "Sanctify them through Your truth. Your word is truth" (John 17:17). This is Jesus' request to God the Father that He use His word to influence believers to live lives set apart for His purposes. Both our lifestyle and our beliefs are to be affected by the Bible, and this requires a humble response of doing the will of God.

James said that what should characterize believers is being "doers of the word and not hearers only" (James 1:22). Self-deception is talking ourselves out of obeying the Bible and therefore cheating ourselves out of the blessings of God that accompany obedience. Some people mark their Bibles, but their Bibles seldom mark them.

Jesus spoke of the blessing of obedience and the foolishness of self-deception when He ended the Sermon on the Mount. He described two types of people, the obedient and disobedient, as builders. The obedient are like the man who built his house on a rock, which enabled the house to stand when the storm came. The disobedient are like the man who built on a foundation of sand and experienced the destruction of his house when the storm came (Matthew 7:24–27). These two people both heard the truth but responded differently. One only *learned* it, while the other truly *lived* it.

CLASSIFICATION

Examining Bible Study Methods

Now [the Bereans] were more noble-minded than those in Thessalonica, for they received the word with great eagerness, examining the Scriptures daily to see whether these things were so.
ACTS 17:11 NASB

All methods of Bible study have value in learning God's Word, but whatever method we use, the point to remember is that *studying the Bible* is what's important. It's to our benefit to pursue the habit of daily reading and studying God's Word.

The usefulness of knowing a variety of Bible study methods is that it helps us be flexible in our approach to scripture as we concentrate on a particular text, subject, or even a word. It also contributes to balancing our learning.

BALANCE

Before looking at different methods of Bible study, some thoughts about being balanced in our study are appropriate.

Old Testament/New Testament

Time spent studying the New Testament should be balanced by study of the Old Testament. It's not surprising that believers living under the new covenant want to spend their time in the New Testament learning about Jesus Christ and His gospel, but the Old Testament is quoted in the New Testament about 250 times. It's been said, "The new is in the old contained, and the old is in the new explained."

When the Bereans were searching the scriptures, they were studying the

Old Testament. The New Testament was in the process of being written at that time. Early Christians had a solid foundation of Old Testament truth, and New Testament truth was added as it gradually became available. This is what's meant by the idea that God's revelation has been progressive.

Doctrine/Christian Living

Another area is balancing the study of Bible doctrine with the study of practical Christian living and how to apply doctrinal truth to everyday life.

Paul's preaching did this. He said to the Ephesian elders, "I have not hesitated to declare to you all the counsel of God" (Acts 20:27). "All the counsel of God" is an inclusive phrase relating to God's revelation covering both doctrine and duty in the Christian life. There was no subject that he intentionally omitted from his teaching. His preaching was well rounded because, in part, he wanted his hearers to be the same.

The point needs to be made that we should be involved in a balanced Bible study plan that uses a variety of techniques. In physical health, eating only those foods that we might enjoy—like snacks and sweets—won't contribute to good health. A balanced diet is required. This is equally true when we study the Bible.

SIX IMPORTANT BIBLE STUDY METHODS

1. The Expositional Method

Expositional Bible study means studying individual Bible books verse by verse, using the observation, interpretation, and application guidelines from chapter 2. The benefit of this method is that it reveals the flow of the author's thoughts throughout the book, which contributes to a more accurate understanding of individual verses. This method requires more thinking about how verses relate to each other but leads to greater understanding in the long run. Bible commentaries are especially helpful with this method.

2. The Survey Method

When we use the survey method, we study Bible books as a whole to become acquainted with general information rather than the details of each verse. We investigate subjects like the author, where he's writing from, his style of writing, the theme, important topics contained in the book, who it was written for, and issues or circumstances the recipients might have been facing. Looking at the political background and chronology of events may explain why certain events happened.

We can also survey the entire Old or New Testament so we understand how the books of the Bible are divided and relate to each other. The thirty-nine Old Testament books, dealing primarily with God's relationship with His chosen nation, Israel, can be divided into five categories:

- Genesis through Deuteronomy, the first five books, are known as the Law or the *Pentateuch* (meaning five volumes).
- Joshua through Esther are the twelve historical books.
- Job through Song of Solomon are the five poetic books.
- Isaiah through Daniel are the five major prophets.
- Hosea through Malachi are the twelve minor prophets.

The twenty-seven New Testament books, originally written in Greek, can be divided into four categories:

- The four Gospels and Acts are the historical books.
- Romans through Philemon, the next thirteen books, are letters of the apostle Paul to churches or individuals.
- Hebrews through Jude, the next eight books, are called the general letters.
- Revelation, a prophetic book, appropriately ends the New Testament.

3. The Topical Method

Occasionally we have a specific topic from the Bible we're interested in studying. We want to accumulate all the Bible says about it and then organize the information. A Bible concordance and a topical Bible guide us to specific verses about topics throughout the Bible. Then we can see how each subject is addressed in the Old Testament and the New Testament, and by individual biblical authors.

4. The Biographical Method

Individual people in the Bible are of interest, so we may want to develop a character sketch. The Bible mentions over twenty-nine hundred people, some by name only. As with a topical method of study, we can use a concordance to find every Bible verse in which the name is found. We have to take care to be sure that the texts all refer to the same person. Six women in the Bible are named Mary, five men are named John, and five men are named James.

Through faith in God's power, believers have accomplished some amazing things. (See Hebrews 11.) These people are examples for us and are called *witnesses*, who testify how God can empower His children to do His will.

God doesn't hide the weaknesses of His servants. David, the man after God's own heart, sinned in the matter of Uriah the Hittite (1 Kings 15:5). The apostle Peter denied the Lord (Matthew 26:69–74). Elijah was a man just like us (James 5:17). This kind of information encourages us. Through their experiences, we learn that God is forgiving and patient and that He is the God of second chances.

5. The Word Study Method

When a person is new to the Christian faith, some terms may be unfamiliar. Words like *propitiation*, *redemption*, *imputation*, *justification*, and *sanctification* are basic to the message of God's salvation in scripture. The words of scripture are the words that God inspired, so they become part of our study. God wants us to understand them. By using a concordance, you'll be able to locate these words and see how they're used.

Several Greek words might be translated into one English word. Using a study tool like *Strong's Exhaustive Concordance* is essential to understanding the variety of meanings. Let's consider a few examples.

The World

Three Greek words all translate into the English word *world*. The Greek word *kosmos* is used in John 3:16: "For God so loved the world that He gave His only begotten Son." This refers to the world order of unsaved people who are opposed to God and controlled by Satan.

The Greek word *aion* is used in Romans 12:2: "And do not be conformed to this world." It refers to the particular age in which we live that's influential with false ideas and evil. J. B. Phillips translates this, "Don't let the world around you squeeze you into its own mould."

The Greek word *oikoumene* is used in Matthew 24:14: "And this gospel of the kingdom shall be preached in all the world." Matthew is referring to the inhabited world of people.

Love

We use the English word *love* for three Greek words that have slightly different meanings. The conversation that the risen Lord Jesus had with Peter in John 21:15–19 uses two of the Greek words.

Since Peter denied knowing the Lord three times, Jesus asked Peter three times if he really loved Him. In the first two questions, Jesus uses the Greek word *agape*, which refers to self-sacrificing love (also used in John 3:16). In Peter's answer he uses another Greek word for love, *phileo*, which emphasizes only fondness, probably because he still feels too much shame to use the word emphasizing a total loving devotion.

When Jesus asks the same question for the third time, He questions even Peter's fondness for Him by also using the word that Peter did, *phileo*. This intentional change of Greek words by Jesus is missed in our English Bible, but it's the reason why Peter was grieved.

Day

Context also has an important bearing on the meaning of words. The word *day*, for example, as used in the Bible, has several meanings that are determined by the context. In Genesis 1:5 there are two meanings: The twelve hours of light are called *day*, and the twenty-four-hour period indicated by the repeated phrase, "the evening and the morning" is also called *day*. When the word *day* appears with a numerical adjective (first day, second day), it consistently refers to a twenty-four-hour period. In Psalm 20:1, *day* refers to an indefinite period of time.

6. The Devotional Method

Many Christians use the phrase "having personal devotions" when referring to the devotional method. This type of study is less technical than the others and is primarily for personal inspiration and encouragement to deepen our relationship with God, drawing near to Him so that He might draw near to us. Bible reading, prayer, and perhaps reading a devotional book with a brief message are normally a part of devotions.

Meditation is a normal part of the devotional method. This is the practice of pondering and reflecting on the meaning of God's words and works and their application to our lives. Anyone who has received a letter from a loved one who is far away understands the meaning of meditation. We read and reread the contents and then think about them. The psalmist said, "I will meditate on Your precepts and consider Your ways" (Psalm 119:15).

The devotional method of study prepares us to meet each day with the knowledge that we have been redeemed by Christ and that He'll strengthen us to do His will.

COLLABORATION

Using Bible Study Helps

When you come, bring with you the cloak that I left at Troas with Carpus and the books, but especially the parchments.
2 Timothy 4:13

Paul, as a Pharisee and as a Christian preacher, was a great student of scripture. No one actually knows what books he was asking Timothy to bring to him when he wrote. But there's a possibility that they were more than books of scripture, that they were books to help him in his own study of scripture.

In this chapter, I'll recommend Bible study tools that are helpful for "a workman" (2 Timothy 2:15). Every worker needs tools of the trade to do his job. The toolbox of Bible students is a personal library, and their tools are study books and helps that aid them in understanding the scriptures. The workshop is that special location where they study.

Study resources produced by Bible scholars give Christians the advantage of reading the insights that these servants of Christ have gained through their own study. Study books are valuable, but they must be kept in their place. They aren't inspired by God as scripture is. They aren't the final word on any biblical text. Our primary source of truth is the Bible. *Sola scriptura* was the Latin saying established during the Protestant Reformation that means "the Bible alone." By using that pronouncement, the Reformers established the Word of God as their only authority for doctrine and practice. God's Word is to be given its rightful place in our lives.

This is an old problem addressed by even the apostle Paul when he asked the Corinthian church, "For while one says, 'I am of Paul,' and another, 'I am of Apollos,' are you not of the flesh?" (1 Corinthians 3:4). We all have our favorite authors, but they should quickly make this same point to not become followers of human beings. The words of people must always be confirmed as being true and not just accepted because of who is saying them.

Study Bibles

As a new believer being invited to a home Bible class, I was amazed to see people with Bibles that had a wealth of additional study notes in them. I had never seen anything like them. I soon purchased a *New Scofield Reference Bible*. When this wore out years later, my next one was a *Ryrie Study Bible*. My wife uses a *MacArthur Study Bible*. Other people I know use the *Life Application Study Bible*. These are only a few in a long list of study Bibles now available in a variety of English translations.

One thing to remember is that the notes in study Bibles are the explanatory words of people, not the authoritative words of God. The study aids are provided as immediate helps and are not meant to be the end of our investigation. We shouldn't depend too heavily on just the explanations in our study Bibles. They'll have helpful introductions to each book of the Bible and outlines so we can see how books fit together. Explanatory notes about the text, doctrine, and Christian living appear on every page. Some study Bibles have charts, articles, extensive cross-references, a concordance, a topical index, and numerous maps.

Bible Dictionaries and Encyclopedias

Among the first tools we need are Bible dictionaries and encyclopedias. They have more than just the definitions of words. They contain brief articles on major Bible subjects with helpful explanations and scripture references related to the subject. These books cover a spectrum of subjects from A to Z, making them reference tools that get used repeatedly. I recommend *The New Unger's Bible Dictionary*, *Zondervan's Pictorial Bible Dictionary*, and *The International Standard Bible Encyclopedia*, a five-volume set.

Exhaustive Concordances

An exhaustive concordance lists every reference where every biblical word is found. When you can remember only a few words of a verse, you can look up one of the words and this book helps you find its reference. Often, in the back, you'll also find an English dictionary for Old Testament Hebrew words and New Testament Greek words. It's important to make sure the concordance you use is keyed to the Bible translation you use. *The Strong's Exhaustive Concordance* is keyed to the King James Version. After my Bible, I use this tool more than any other resource that I have.

Topical Bibles

Topical Bibles list biblical words alphabetically and give select references to where the word you are looking for is found. Many times the entire verse is written out so you can read the verse in the book. Larger subjects are broken down into subcategories so you can find verses with a particular emphasis. For example, in *Nave's Topical Bible*, the word *faith* has the following subheadings: faith enjoined; faith exemplified; faith in Christ; and the trial of faith. Use this resource when you're doing word studies or character sketches.

Expository Dictionaries

When studying words of the Bible, use an expository dictionary. A Webster's English dictionary is fine as far as it goes, but it primarily deals with English. We're dealing with English translations of Greek words when we study the New Testament. This study aid examines the original Greek words used in verses and then gives a brief definition and explanation of the word. It also has select references to where the Greek word appears in the New Testament. I recommend *Vine's Expository Dictionary of Old and New Testament Words* by W. E. Vine.

Bible Atlases

For those who want a more detailed description of geography in the Bible with explanatory articles, this is the book to use. Atlases contain many more maps than those that appear in the backs of Bibles. This resource won't be used as frequently as others, but it helps to better understand locations and travel in Bible times.

Commentaries

This is my favorite category of study helps. Most of the books I own are commentaries. Using these books is like being taught by great men and women of God.

Some are expository in nature, explaining individual verses and analyzing how they fit together. These generally include an outline of the entire book of the Bible. Other commentaries are more devotional, emphasizing lessons for Christian living. Some are technical in nature, working closely with the original languages.

After you read several commentaries, you'll soon discover that the books with more pages are normally more helpful because they address more issues. Difficult questions that arise are usually addressed, including possible solutions.

Of course, commentaries aren't the final word about any text. Even Bible scholars disagree at times. My humble experience has been that I find myself not agreeing with any Bible commentator 100 percent of the time. My guess is that this is the conclusion of most serious students of the Bible.

Books that have been helpful to me are single books that cover the entire Bible like *Jamieson, Fausset, and Brown's Commentary on the Whole Bible* (that's one book!). Sets that cover the entire New Testament or the entire Bible (which provide greater detail) include the six-volume set of Matthew Henry commentaries; *The Bible Knowledge Commentary* by Walvoord and Zuck, a two-volume set; and *The Bible Exposition Commentary* by Warren Wiersbe, a six-volume set. Much larger sets are the New Testament Commentary series by Hendriksen and Kistemaker and the MacArthur New Testament Commentary series.

GETTING BIBLE STUDY RESOURCES

I want to say a few things about where to get Bible study tools. Every Christian should own a few basic study books. To develop your personal library, make a wish list of the books you need. I've learned the hard way not to buy books I'm not acquainted with. The money I used to buy ten books that weren't that good could have been used to buy one good book.

Add the study tools to your library that are valuable to you. Get recommendations from Christians who you believe can help you with this project and then visit your local Christian bookstore or an Internet bookseller.

You can also borrow Bible study books from your church library or even many public libraries. If the public library lacks a title you're seeking, it might be able to order the book from another library.

The Internet offers a wealth of free Bible study tools. Here's a list of reputable Web sites in random order with brief descriptions:

bible.org

You'll find articles by topic or by passage. They have online Bible dictionaries, concordances, encyclopedias, and an extensive question-and-answer section.

crosswalk.com

Offers commentaries, concordances, dictionaries, and encyclopedias.

studylight.org

Featuring daily devotionals, commentaries, concordances, dictionaries, and sermon helps.

preceptaustin.org

Bible commentaries with verse-by-verse exposition, dictionaries, and maps are available.

ccel.org

CCEL stands for the Christian Classics Ethereal Library. Includes many works from Christian thinkers throughout history.

biblebb.com

Includes sermons and articles by great preachers from the past, and a lengthy question-and-answer list.

CHAPTER 5

MOTIVATION

Putting Thoughts into Action

You therefore, beloved, knowing this beforehand, be on your guard so that you are not carried away by the error of unscrupulous people and lose your own firm commitment, but grow in the grace and knowledge of our Lord and Savior Jesus Christ. To Him be the glory, both now and to the day of eternity. Amen.

2 Peter 3:17–18 NASB

Many people have made their Bibles "personal" by the comments they've written in them year after year. It's hard for some people to think about replacing their old Bibles with new ones even if they're falling apart—because they've found such wisdom, comfort, and power in the pages they've studied and cherished for years.

Alan Redpath, pastor of Moody Church in Chicago from 1953 to 1962, advised believers to "wreck" their Bibles every ten years. He meant to wear them out by constant use. I once saw a message on a church sign that read, "A Bible that is falling apart is usually owned by someone who isn't." This is a point well taken.

I imagine most believers would say that reading and studying the Bible is a good thing to do. Virtually all Christian families in the United States own at least one Bible. The Bible is repeatedly the bestselling book every year. . .but perhaps still one of the least read. Why the disconnect? The answer has both a human dimension and a spiritual one.

OVERCOMING HINDRANCES

From a human perspective, the busyness of life can keep us from scripture. Sometimes, we can be lazy when it comes to our spiritual health and responsibilities. And sometimes, we simply don't understand how important Bible study actually is.

From a spiritual perspective, sin in our lives can keep us from spending time in the Word. We can lose our spiritual appetite for the knowledge of God. The forces of darkness are doing all they can to keep us from studying God's truth. Any activity that uses up our time will do—it doesn't have to be evil, just something that weighs us down and takes our time.

We might ask, "Isn't going to church enough? Isn't reading and studying the Bible what pastors and Sunday school teachers do?" It's true that this is a large part of what pastors and teachers are to do, but it's also what everyone in a church congregation is supposed to do. Consider these verses, all of which we've already referenced:

Now these people [the Bereans] were more noble-minded than those in Thessalonica, for they received the word with great eagerness, examining the Scriptures daily to see whether these things were so.
ACTS 17:11 NASB

For whatever was written in earlier times was written for our instruction.
ROMANS 15:4 NASB

Study to show yourself approved to God, a workman who does not need to be ashamed, rightly dividing the word of truth.
2 TIMOTHY 2:15

As he ended his second letter, the apostle Peter strongly urged believers to "grow...in the knowledge of our Lord and Savior Jesus Christ" (2 Peter 3:18), something that starts with knowing His Word.

MARY AND MARTHA

As we conclude, let's consider the lives of Mary and Martha of Bethany. Mary is a great biblical example of a person whose desire was to be taught by Jesus: Every time she appears in the Bible, she's kneeling before Him. In John 11, she's at His feet in sorrow. In John 12, she's at His feet in adoration. In Luke 10, she's at His feet to learn truth. Mary, the worshipper, wants her soul fed by Jesus; her sister Martha, the worker, wants to feed Jesus.

Mary and Martha had welcomed Jesus into their home. With good intentions, Martha took steps to prepare a meal for the honored guest. Mary is now introduced into the story: "And she had a sister called Mary, who also sat at Jesus' feet and heard His word" (Luke 10:39). Martha was in the kitchen cooking food, and Mary was in the living room learning from Jesus. Martha, annoyed that Mary wasn't helping with the work, interrupted the Lord, saying, "Lord, do You not care that my sister has left me to serve alone? Therefore tell her to help me" (Luke 10:40).

Jesus, in His divine wisdom, analyzed the situation and told Martha she was filled with unnecessary anxiety that had harmfully affected her priorities. The things she worried about really weren't important. "One thing is needed," Jesus told Martha, "and Mary has chosen that good part, which shall not be taken away from her" (Luke 10:42).

Jesus commended Mary for having good priorities—namely, learning the Word of God. Bible expositor G. Campbell Morgan calls this "the one supreme necessity."

Mary's experience was that of being taught by the incarnate Christ. Each of us can experience the blessing of being taught by the risen Christ—by the power of His Holy Spirit, through the study of God's amazing Word.

Grow in the grace and knowledge of our Lord
and Savior Jesus Christ. To Him be the glory,
both now and to the day of eternity. Amen.
2 Peter 3:18 NASB

STUDY TOPIC:

DATE:

STUDY TOPIC:

DATE:

STUDY TOPIC:

DATE:

STUDY TOPIC:

DATE:

STUDY TOPIC:

DATE:

STUDY TOPIC: ....

DATE: ....

STUDY TOPIC:

DATE:

STUDY TOPIC: ....

DATE: ....

STUDY TOPIC:

DATE:

STUDY TOPIC:

DATE:

STUDY TOPIC:

DATE:

STUDY TOPIC:

DATE:

STUDY TOPIC:

DATE:

STUDY TOPIC:

DATE:

STUDY TOPIC:

DATE:

STUDY TOPIC:

DATE:

STUDY TOPIC:

DATE:

STUDY TOPIC:

DATE:

STUDY TOPIC:

DATE:

STUDY TOPIC:

DATE:

STUDY TOPIC:

DATE:

STUDY TOPIC:

DATE:

STUDY TOPIC:

DATE:

STUDY TOPIC:

DATE:

STUDY TOPIC:

DATE:

STUDY TOPIC: ....

DATE: ....

STUDY TOPIC: ....

DATE: ....

STUDY TOPIC:

DATE:

STUDY TOPIC:

DATE:

STUDY TOPIC:

DATE:

STUDY TOPIC:

DATE:

STUDY TOPIC:

DATE:

STUDY TOPIC:

DATE:

STUDY TOPIC:

DATE:

STUDY TOPIC: ....

DATE: ....

STUDY TOPIC:

DATE:

STUDY TOPIC:

DATE:

STUDY TOPIC:

DATE:

STUDY TOPIC: ....

DATE: ....

STUDY TOPIC:

DATE:

STUDY TOPIC: ....

DATE: ....

STUDY TOPIC: ....

DATE: ....

STUDY TOPIC:

DATE:

STUDY TOPIC:

DATE:

STUDY TOPIC:

DATE:

STUDY TOPIC:

DATE:

STUDY TOPIC:

DATE:

STUDY TOPIC:

DATE:

STUDY TOPIC:

DATE:

STUDY TOPIC:

DATE:

STUDY TOPIC: ....

DATE: ....

STUDY TOPIC:

DATE:

STUDY TOPIC:

DATE:

STUDY TOPIC:

DATE:

STUDY TOPIC: ....

DATE: ....

STUDY TOPIC:

DATE:

STUDY TOPIC:

DATE:

STUDY TOPIC:

DATE:

STUDY TOPIC:

DATE:

STUDY TOPIC:

DATE:

STUDY TOPIC: ....

DATE: ....

STUDY TOPIC:

DATE:

STUDY TOPIC:

DATE:

STUDY TOPIC:

DATE:

STUDY TOPIC:

DATE:

STUDY TOPIC:

DATE:

STUDY TOPIC:

DATE:

STUDY TOPIC:

DATE:

STUDY TOPIC:

DATE:

STUDY TOPIC:

DATE:

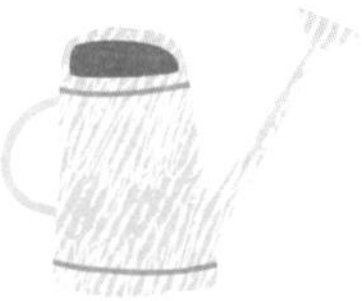

STUDY TOPIC:

DATE:

STUDY TOPIC:

DATE:

STUDY TOPIC:

DATE:

STUDY TOPIC: ....

DATE: ....

STUDY TOPIC:

DATE:

STUDY TOPIC:

DATE:

STUDY TOPIC: ....

DATE: ....

STUDY TOPIC:

DATE:

STUDY TOPIC:

DATE:

STUDY TOPIC:

DATE:

STUDY TOPIC:

DATE:

STUDY TOPIC:

DATE:

STUDY TOPIC: ....

DATE: ....

STUDY TOPIC:

DATE:

STUDY TOPIC:

DATE:

STUDY TOPIC:

DATE:

STUDY TOPIC:

DATE:

STUDY TOPIC:

DATE:

STUDY TOPIC: ....

DATE: ....

STUDY TOPIC:

DATE:

STUDY TOPIC: ……………………………………

DATE: ……………………………………

STUDY TOPIC:

DATE:

STUDY TOPIC: ....

DATE: ....

STUDY TOPIC:

DATE:

STUDY TOPIC:

DATE:

STUDY TOPIC:

DATE:

STUDY TOPIC:

DATE:

STUDY TOPIC:

DATE:

STUDY TOPIC:

DATE:

STUDY TOPIC:

DATE:

STUDY TOPIC:

DATE:

STUDY TOPIC:

DATE:

STUDY TOPIC:

DATE:

STUDY TOPIC:

DATE:

STUDY TOPIC:

DATE:

STUDY TOPIC:

DATE:

STUDY TOPIC:

DATE:

STUDY TOPIC:

DATE:

STUDY TOPIC: ....

DATE: ....

STUDY TOPIC:

DATE:

STUDY TOPIC:

DATE:

STUDY TOPIC:

DATE:

STUDY TOPIC:

DATE:

STUDY TOPIC:

DATE:

STUDY TOPIC:

DATE:

STUDY TOPIC:

DATE:

STUDY TOPIC:

DATE:

STUDY TOPIC:

DATE:

STUDY TOPIC:

DATE:

STUDY TOPIC:

DATE:

STUDY TOPIC:

DATE:

STUDY TOPIC:

DATE:

STUDY TOPIC:

DATE:

STUDY TOPIC: ....

DATE: ....

STUDY TOPIC:

DATE:

STUDY TOPIC:

DATE:

STUDY TOPIC: ....

DATE: ....

STUDY TOPIC:

DATE:

STUDY TOPIC:

DATE:

STUDY TOPIC:

DATE:

STUDY TOPIC:

DATE:

STUDY TOPIC:

DATE:

STUDY TOPIC:

DATE:

STUDY TOPIC:

DATE:

STUDY TOPIC:

DATE:

STUDY TOPIC:

DATE:

STUDY TOPIC:

DATE:

STUDY TOPIC:

DATE:

STUDY TOPIC: ....

DATE: ....

STUDY TOPIC:

DATE:

STUDY TOPIC:

DATE:

STUDY TOPIC:

DATE:

STUDY TOPIC:

DATE:

STUDY TOPIC:

DATE:

STUDY TOPIC:

DATE:

STUDY TOPIC:

DATE:

STUDY TOPIC:

DATE:

STUDY TOPIC:

DATE:

STUDY TOPIC:

DATE:

STUDY TOPIC: ....

DATE: ....

STUDY TOPIC: ....

DATE: ....

STUDY TOPIC:

DATE:

STUDY TOPIC: ....

DATE: ....

STUDY TOPIC:

DATE:

STUDY TOPIC:

DATE: